The
Spirit
of
WORKMANSHIP

Akin Akinyemi

SYNCTERFACE™
Syncterface Media
London
www.syncterfacemedia.com

THE SPIRIT OF WORKMANSHIP

ISBN: 978-0-9569741-2-9
Copyright © March 2012 by Akin Akinyemi
Revised Edition: December 2020
All Rights Reserved

Published in the United Kingdom by

SYNCTERFACE

Syncterface Media
London

www.syncterfacemedia.com
info@syncterfacemedia.com

Cover Design by Syncterface Media

Contents

1

The Spirit Of

*L*earning about the Holy Spirit is always an exciting exercise for me. The Holy Spirit is not only a member of the trinity that we have operating on the earth today. He is also the one that reveals the Father and the Son to us. Every encounter with Him or His works is always an explosive one to the mind. Without Him, we cannot know or understand the things of God. What He reveals goes beyond intellectual knowledge; it is the knowledge that enters the heart as a seed seeking to grow to maturity, this is why I was excited when He gave me an understanding of what I called "THE SPIRIT OF."

While at a prayer meeting, the person leading the session asked us to pray using the prayer of Apostle Paul for the Ephesian Church in Ephesians 1:15-20.

> *15Wherefore I also, after I heard of your faith in the Lord Jesus, and love unto all the saints,*
>
> *16Cease not to give thanks for you, making mention of you*

in my prayers;

[17]That the God of our Lord Jesus Christ, the Father of glory, may give unto you the spirit of wisdom and revelation in the knowledge of him: [18]The eyes of your understanding being enlightened; that ye may know what is the hope of his calling, and what the riches of the glory of his inheritance in the saints,

[19]And what is the exceeding greatness of his power to us-ward who believe, according to the working of his mighty power,

[20]Which he wrought in Christ, when he raised him from the dead, and set him at his own right hand in the heavenly places,

Ephesians 1:15-20

I finished reading these verses and read it a few more times (*as I normally do when reading scriptures*) when suddenly I heard the voice of the Spirit in my heart about *Verse 17*. He said to me, "Did you notice that Paul did not pray for Wisdom and Revelation?"

[17]That the God of our Lord Jesus Christ, the Father of glory, may give unto you the spirit of wisdom and revelation in the knowledge of him:

I paused for a moment as I did not get what He was saying and had to read a few more times before I noticed it. He prayed that "*God...... may give unto you THE SPIRIT OF wisdom and revelation*" It still took a while for me to get it even after this. It was not until He spoke again and said, "*It is one thing for you to be a consumer of wise counsel, it is another thing for you to be a generator of wise counsel.*"

Too many of us, Christians, are consumers of

wisdom and revelation (which is not a bad thing) but what have you received yourselves from the Holy Spirit? We draw more confidence from the truths we discover ourselves than we do from what we hear from others. God's illumination of His word in your heart is a direct response of heaven to you. Wisdom and Revelation are products of the Spirit of wisdom and the Spirit of revelation. It is the Spirit that generates "the product." Wow! This Spirit of Revelation takes the cover off the hidden knowledge of God, so we gain an understanding relevant for exploits. This revelation of knowledge is the food that feeds the God nature that is now resident in the born-again Christian.

As soon as I saw this, I had to share it with others in the prayer meeting as it was fresh from the Holy Spirit. As I have now come to understand, every revelation you get from God is not only a seed that needs to grow in the heart; it is also an open the door to more profound things of God. Where else in the Bible had I missed "THE SPIRIT OF"? Where had I concentrated on the product rather than the source?

Studying this concept has been one of the most exciting and explosive studies of the Word of God I have engaged in in a long time. Using a concordance, I combed the bible from Genesis to Revelation to find everywhere there was a reference to the "THE SPIRIT OF" something. After categorisation, I found more than thirty different references including the Spirit of God, the Spirit of the Lord, the Spirit of Truth, the Spirit of Understanding, the Spirit of Wisdom, the Spirit of Knowledge, the Spirit of Counsel, the Spirit of Prophecy and many more.

As I meditated on this, I thought, but there is only one Holy Spirit, so what does this mean? Praise God, He always answers the sincere questions of the heart but in my case, for the most of the time, He asks questions that expose my ignorance and fills me with knowledge. So He asked me, *"When a man and a woman get married, are they one?"* I quickly ran through the scriptures in my mind and remembered this scripture in Genesis.

> [24]*Therefore shall a man leave his father and his mother, and shall cleave unto his wife: and they shall be one flesh.*
>
> *Genesis 2:24*

So I answered God and said, *"They are one."* He then asked me, *"Is the manifestation of the wife the same as the manifestation of the husband?"* I got the point. It is one Holy Spirit, but the manifestation of His person varies. Notice that I said *"the manifestation of His person."* A lot of Christians only know the Holy Spirit by the manifestation of His gifts.

> [1]*Now concerning spiritual gifts, brethren, I would not have you ignorant.*
>
> [2]*Ye know that ye were Gentiles, carried away unto these dumb idols, even as ye were led.*
>
> [3]*Wherefore I give you to understand, that no man speaking by the Spirit of God calleth Jesus accursed: and that no man can say that Jesus is the Lord, but by the Holy Ghost.*
>
> [4]*Now there are diversities of gifts, but the same Spirit.*
>
> [5]*And there are differences of administrations, but the same Lord.* [6]*And there are diversities of operations, but it is the same God which worketh all in all.*
>
> [7]*But the manifestation of the Spirit is given to every man*

to profit withal.

[8]For to one is given by the Spirit the word of wisdom; to another the word of knowledge by the same Spirit;

[9]To another faith by the same Spirit; to another the gifts of healing by the same Spirit;

[10]To another the working of miracles; to another prophecy; to another discerning of spirits; to another divers kinds of tongues; to another the interpretation of tongues:

[11]But all these worketh that one and the selfsame Spirit, dividing to every man severally as he will.

1 Corinthians 12:1-11

Can you imagine if a child's only way of describing their parents is by the gifts the child gets on special occasions? That is how limiting our understanding of the Holy Spirit will be if we do not seek to understand His person.

[4]Now there are diversities of gifts, but the same Spirit.

[5]And there are differences of administrations, but the same Lord. [6]And there are diversities of operations, but it is the same God which worketh all in all.

[7]But the manifestation of the Spirit is given to every man to profit withal.

[11]But all these worketh that one and the selfsame Spirit, dividing to every man severally as he will.

1 Corinthians 12:4-7,11

There are different manifestations of the gifts but the same Holy Spirit. These gifts manifest as the Holy Spirit chooses, and we do not have control over when the manifestations occur, but what do we have when the gifts are not manifesting? We have the indwelling of His person that lives permanently in us.

Naming the Spirits

Good or bad spirits are named after the manifestation they bring. For example, when we look through scriptures, a deaf spirit will not cause blindness, and a blind spirit will not cause deafness. In like manner, you can have a greater awareness of some of these spirits more than others. The depth of understanding you have of these spirits determines the degree to which you will allow the spirit to flow through you. You will notice in scriptures that every time a specific spirit is named, the manifestation that follows is in line with the spirit in operation. For example, in the story of the Hebrew boys in the book of Daniel, the spirit of knowledge was in operation, so they were ten times better than the other children. I talked about this in detail in the book "The Knowledge of the Hebrew Boys."

Spirits generally bring a supernatural ability to the human body. They drive the body to do unexpected things. They push the body into limitless dimensions, so we see statements like "the spirit entered me, The Spirit of the Lord came upon me, and they were filled with the Spirit" and many more. After these statements, we always see one divine act or the other take place. This action that takes place after the Holy Spirit presses through our spirits into the physical is significant because it demonstrates a fundamental fact about the Holy Spirit.

He manifests "quicker" when there is a vision broken down into goals. People with God-given ideas who break them down into goals are more likely to trigger the spirit than those who have no vision or clearly defined goals.

> ²*And the LORD answered me, and said, Write the vision, and make it plain upon tables, that he may run that readeth it.*

> *Habakkuk 2:2*

Now, there is a significant difference between the good spirits and the bad spirits. The good spirits respect your will while the bad ones, in most cases, override your will. So be careful, every spirit that wants to override your will is not from God.

We will, in this book, look at all the manifestations of "THE SPIRIT OF" that I found in the bible. I will focus only on the good spirits to keep things in context. What has, for me, been interesting is the fact that when we put all the "spirits of" together, they cover almost every area of life. What is even more exciting is the fact that the manifestation of His person belongs to every Christian and I do not have to think that I may not be "anointed" to operate in a particular gift or stand in a particular ministry. As long as you have and accept that the Holy Spirit is in you, every one of the spirits we will look at is available to you. To deny any one of them is to deny the Holy Spirit Himself.

Chapter Key Points

It is one thing for you to be a consumer of wise counsel, it is another thing for you to be a generator of wise counsel

This revelation of knowledge is the food that feeds the God nature that is now resident in the born-again Christian

The Holy Spirit manifests "quicker" when there is a vision broken down into goals

2

The Spirit of Workmanship

*T*he Spirit of Workmanship is one of the spirits rarely talked about when we talk about the Spirits of God. As I mentioned in the previous chapter, everywhere you see the spirit of "something", find out what the product of the spirit is. This spirit of workmanship is an interesting one because it is not used frequently in the scriptures. What exactly is workmanship?

The Collins English Dictionary defines workmanship as *"the art or skill of a workman," "the art or skill with which something is made or executed," "the degree of art or skill exhibited in the finished product"* and *"the piece of work so produced."* The Hebrew translation, on the other hand, gives a fascinating perspective to the word in *Exodus 31:3.*

> *¹And the LORD spake unto Moses, saying,*
>
> *²See, I have called by name Bezaleel the son of Uri, the son of Hur, of the tribe of Judah:*

> *³And I have filled him with the spirit of God, in wisdom, and in understanding, and in knowledge, and in all manner of workmanship,*
>
> *Exodus 31:3*

The word "*workmanship*," from Strong's concordance, could be rendered as "*sent as a messenger to deputise in skilful execution in occupation, business or industry.*" From these three verses in Exodus, we can answer a few questions that this rendition will no doubt raise. Firstly, who is doing the sending? It is clear from Verse 1 that the Lord that is speaking to Moses is one doing the "*sending*" and the one for whom a "*deputy*" is being appointed. Secondly, who is the messenger being talked about here? *Verse 2* again clearly shows that a man called Bezaleel is the one deputising for God. We will not cover it in this book, but there is a crucial point in *Verse 2* that needs to be raised here. Bezaleel is filled with "THE SPIRIT OF GOD." This is important because there is a pattern in scriptures everywhere "THE SPIRIT OF GOD" is used.

This definition of workmanship shows us at least three places where the spirit of workmanship operates. He operates in occupation, business and industry. Occupation here relates to the employee. So the spirit of workmanship operates in the employee, the business and the industry. Notice in *Verse 3* that it is only the spirit of workmanship that has "ALL MANNER." This ensures that any employee, business and industry are covered by the operation of the spirit.

The manifestations of the Spirit that many Christians have limited to the pulpit should also manifest in the employee while at work, the business and the industry in which the Christian works. I remember the story a brother once told me. This brother, though a pastor, does a lot of work with corporations in the area of human resources and talent development. According to his story, he had just finished a talk to a group of business executives who did not know that he was also a pastor. One of the executives walked up to him and told him there was something he was not telling this executive and the audience. The brother thought he had missed something, but the executive said: "*You must be a pastor because the same thing I feel when in Church, I am feeling in this meeting room.*" God is as interested in what you do outside Church as He is in what you do inside Church. In any case, how can we truly serve God if some areas are off-limits to Him?

The Spirit of Workmanship is a creative spirit that is in operation in the creation of products, businesses and industries for the advancement of humanity. Remember workmanship also means "finished product." The Bible tells us we are God's finished product.

> *10For we are his workmanship, created in Christ Jesus unto good works, which God hath before ordained that we should walk in them.*
>
> *Ephesians 2:10*

We are a product of God's workmanship. When we look at how intricate, and precise the workings of the human body is, those of us who believe in creation cannot but conclude that there must have been an intelligent mind at work in the creation of the body.

I came across some interesting facts about this body on the Internet. I came across some points worth sharing, even though scientists have different views. Here are some of the intricate workings of the body that I came across.

1. The brain, with billions of nerve cells, has more processing capacity than any computer ever built by man. Brain signals, in response to stimuli, have been known to move at over 100 miles per hour. The brain also acts as some data storage tank holding information about the body structure which causes a phenomenon called "phantom pain" that causes an amputee to feel pain in a body part that is no longer physically there.

2. Some scholars have described the tongue as one of the strongest muscles in the body. Like our fingerprints, it is unique in print to every individual. I also came across the story of one of Adolf Hitler's henchmen who, some claim, Israeli agents identified by the print of his ears.

3. Some have classed the eyes as the second most complex organ of the body. The average person blinks about 10,000 times per day. According to the Bible, one blink is long enough for you to miss the end of the world. The eye can focus on more than 40 things per second and contributes more than 80 per cent of your knowledge intake. In some instances, some have said that the eye can see candlelight up to 10 miles away.

Is it not amazing what God has created from dust? Who would have thought that dust as a raw material could produce products with such levels of complexity.

> *⁷And the LORD God formed man of the dust of the ground, and breathed into his nostrils the breath of life; and man became a living soul.*

Genesis 2:7

It is the knowledge in the mind of a creator that determines the dimension of possibilities open to the creator, not the availability of raw materials. I believe if we have the fullness of the knowledge in the mind of God, we can take dust and recreate every organ in the human body for use in the replacement of defective ones. Initially, this may sound far-fetched, but look at what Jesus did.

> *¹And as Jesus passed by, he saw a man which was blind from his birth. ²And his disciples asked him, saying, Master, who did sin, this man, or his parents, that he was born blind?*

> *³Jesus answered, Neither hath this man sinned, nor his parents: but that the works of God should be made manifest in him.*

> *⁴I must work the works of him that sent me, while it is day: the night cometh, when no man can work.*

> *⁵As long as I am in the world, I am the light of the world.*

> *⁶When he had thus spoken, he spat on the ground, and made clay of the spittle, and he anointed the eyes of the blind man with the clay, ⁷And said unto him, Go, wash in the pool of Siloam, (which is by interpretation, Sent.) He went his way therefore, and washed, and came seeing.*

> *⁸The neighbours therefore, and they which before had seen him that he was blind, said, Is not this he that sat and begged?*

⁹Some said, This is he: others said, He is like him: but he said, I am he.

¹⁰Therefore said they unto him, How were thine eyes opened?

¹¹He answered and said, A man that is called Jesus made clay, and anointed mine eyes, and said unto me, Go to the pool of Siloam, and wash: and I went and washed, and I received sight.

John 9:1-11

I believe this man may have either been missing eyeballs or had eyeballs that were not formed at the time he was born, therefore being blind from birth. If Jesus could do this, then every believer should be able to do the same thing. Even now, it is possible to him that believes.

Let me remind you that somewhere around you is the raw material you need to create your future. The limitation of humanity has always been in the mind and not the raw material. The shortage of raw material is always a trigger for creativity in a mind lined up with God. No dream dies due to lack of raw materials. Dreams die when minds stop functioning right. Dreams in dead minds are never born, and dreams die when they come in contact with dead minds. So be careful the mind you share your dream with.

The concept of light in the mind is one of the reasons for the gospel. The Gospel of Christ is the light that enlightens the mind and allows the mind to enter into the creative dimension of God. In case you think this last example was a mistake, look at another story of what Jesus did with what you can again refer to as "dust."

> ⁵When Jesus then lifted up his eyes, and saw a great company come unto him, he saith unto Philip, Whence shall we buy bread, that these may eat?

> ⁶And this he said to prove him: for he himself knew what he would do. ⁷Philip answered him, Two hundred pennyworth of bread is not sufficient for them, that every one of them may take a little.

> ⁸One of his disciples, Andrew, Simon Peter's brother, saith unto him, ⁹There is a lad here, which hath five barley loaves, and two small fishes: but what are they among so many?

> ¹⁰And Jesus said, Make the men sit down. Now there was much grass in the place. So the men sat down, in number about five thousand.

> ¹¹And Jesus took the loaves; and when he had given thanks, he distributed to the disciples, and the disciples to them that were set down; and likewise of the fishes as much as they would.

> ¹²When they were filled, he said unto his disciples, Gather up the fragments that remain, that nothing be lost.

> ¹³Therefore they gathered them together, and filled twelve baskets with the fragments of the five barley loaves, which remained over and above unto them that had eaten.

> ¹⁴Then those men, when they had seen the miracle that Jesus did, said, This is of a truth that prophet that should come into the world.

> *John 6:5-14*

I urge you, right now, take a few seconds, break and reset your possibility paradigm. Think of the many things you want to do and maybe have left undone because you thought you did not have the right raw materials. Bring these all under the classification I call "dust" and from this dust begin to create the future you want in your mind. Remember what Jesus said.

23Jesus said unto him, If thou canst believe, all things are possible to him that believeth.

Mark 9:23

If God can from dust make this complex machine called the human body, the believers deputising for Him can equally be as effective if we let the spirit of workmanship flow through us.

The Manifestation of the Spirit

Bezaleel was not just filled with the Spirit because God felt like it. God filled him for a purpose. This purpose was the evidence of the inward work that God had done.

1And the LORD spake unto Moses, saying,

2See, I have called by name Bezaleel the son of Uri, the son of Hur, of the tribe of Judah:

3And I have filled him with the spirit of God, in wisdom, and in understanding, and in knowledge, and in all manner of workmanship, 4To devise cunning works, to work in gold, and in silver, and in brass,

5And in cutting of stones, to set them, and in carving of timber, to work in all manner of workmanship.

Exodus 31:1-5

The infilling of Bezaleel was for three primary activities of devising, working and cutting. Devising here gives you the ability to invent, compute and forecast from mental effort. You can create your original design of things following the pattern you see in your spirit. That idea in your mind is also a great idea. Every great product was once an untested idea in the mind of its creator. They only went the extra mile and overcame all the "what if's."

Working allows you to generate results industrially. You can apply your effort to push goals in an industrialised way. Remember what Jesus did with the young boy's lunch when he multiplied it and fed five thousand people with it. Think global but start local, and the supernatural breath of God will multiply the works of your hand many times over.

Cutting is the act of using mechanical tools to achieve goals. It refers to the use of technology or technologically driven platforms to deliver your work. See the example of Uzziah in the Bible.

> *5And he sought God in the days of Zechariah, who had understanding in the visions of God: and as long as he sought the LORD, God made him to prosper.*
>
> *6And he went forth and warred against the Philistines, and brake down the wall of Gath, and the wall of Jabneh, and the wall of Ashdod, and built cities about Ashdod, and among the Philistines.*
>
> *7And God helped him against the Philistines, and against the Arabians that dwelt in Gurbaal, and the Mehunims.*
>
> *8And the Ammonites gave gifts to Uzziah: and his name spread abroad even to the entering in of Egypt; for he strengthened himself exceedingly.*
>
> *9Moreover Uzziah built towers in Jerusalem at the corner gate, and at the valley gate, and at the turning of the wall, and fortified them. 10Also he built towers in the desert, and digged many wells: for he had much cattle, both in*

the low country, and in the plains: husbandmen also, and vine dressers in the mountains, and in Carmel: for he loved husbandry.

[11]Moreover Uzziah had an host of fighting men, that went out to war by bands, according to the number of their account by the hand of Jeiel the scribe and Maaseiah the ruler, under the hand of Hananiah, one of the king's captains.

[12]The whole number of the chief of the fathers of the mighty men of valour were two thousand and six hundred.

[13]And under their hand was an army, three hundred thousand and seven thousand and five hundred, that made war with mighty power, to help the king against the enemy.

[14]And Uzziah prepared for them throughout all the host shields, and spears, and helmets, and habergeons, and bows, and slings to cast stones.

[15]And he made in Jerusalem engines, invented by cunning men, to be on the towers and upon the bulwarks, to shoot arrows and great stones withal. And his name spread far abroad; for he was marvellously helped, till he was strong.

2 Chronicles 26:5-15

Uzziah and his men invented engines as long as He recognised God as the source of all. This dimension of creativity is what the Spirit of Workmanship is about. What is the technology of your day that pushes things forward? The internet is one that comes to mind as it can bring an idea to market in record time. You do not have to reject the internet because of the risk of negative information and its destructive capability. Which tool is not double-edged? Most tools are not bad in themselves. There is nothing wrong with a knife when used in the kitchen by a chef. However, a gangster can cause untold grief by using the same knife to stab someone else.

Do not despise technology. It gives you an edge and makes you more productive.

Chapter Key Points

It is the knowledge in the mind of a creator that determines the dimension of possibilities open to the creator, not the availability of raw materials

No dream dies due to lack of raw materials. Dreams die when minds stop functioning right

Every great product was once an untested idea in its creator's mind

3

The Principle of Work - I

Work is an exciting thing. Work is something you expend spiritual, mental and physical energy on to deliver products or services. Every true expression of work for a Christian should contain activities in the spirit, mind and body. Man and the world are an expression of the work and workmanship of God. Work is spiritual to engage in whether behind a pulpit or not. The first revelation of God we have in scriptures is that of a working God who actively created products that revealed Him and continue to reveal Him to humanity.

> *[1]Thus the heavens and the earth were finished, and all the host of them.*
>
> *[2]And on the seventh day God ended his work which he had made; and he rested on the seventh day from all his work which he had made.*
>
> *Genesis 2:1-2*

Work in any of the dimensions mentioned requires a degree of exertion. When God rested, He "*stopped exertion,*" so there is a certain degree of "*exertion*" involved in what God did. He was like a woman giving birth. There is a type of travail engaged in giving birth and nurturing what is born. I believe the fundamental spring of work comes from the spirit. When a person has an internal disconnection with the spirit, they lose focus, and they expend their mental and physical energy in unproductive ways. When we expend energy without direction, we create societal confusion that if uncontrolled, will diminish or destroy productivity.

Several things contribute to determining whether work is exciting or not, whether the exertion involved is worth paying the price for or not.

An Understanding of the End Product

I worked for an organisation, many years ago, that acquired lots of companies but did not deliver the desired value from the acquisitions. My curious mind sought to find an answer to the challenge. I found some complaints from people that I believe are consistent with what transpires when projects fail.

Resources say things like "*Nobody tells us anything around here,*" "*I don't even know how relevant my task is to the whole.*" Statements like this reduce creativity in an individual. Highly productive resources are productive on purpose. They engage in planned activities which may be painful or unexciting, but because they have a goal before them that they believe, the work gets done anyway.

6Who, being in the form of God, thought it not robbery to be equal with God:

7But made himself of no reputation, and took upon him the form of a servant, and was made in the likeness of men:

8And being found in fashion as a man, he humbled himself, and became obedient unto death, even the death of the cross.

9Wherefore God also hath highly exalted him, and given him a name which is above every name:

10That at the name of Jesus every knee should bow, of things in heaven, and things in earth, and things under the earth;

Philippians 2:6-10

6Who, although being essentially one with God and in the form of God [possessing the fullness of the attributes which make God God], did not think this equality with God was a thing to be eagerly grasped or retained,

7But stripped Himself [of all privileges and rightful dignity], so as to assume the guise of a servant (slave), in that He became like men and was born a human being.

8And after He had appeared in human form, He abased and humbled Himself [still further] and carried His obedience to the extreme of death, even the death of the cross!

9Therefore [because He stooped so low] God has highly exalted Him and has freely bestowed on Him the name that is above every name, 10That in (at) the name of Jesus every knee should (must) bow, in heaven and on earth and under the earth,

Philippians 2:6-10 (AMP)

Jesus stooped so low for the goal of humanity rising so high. Many have lost high and lofty dreams because the carriers failed to humble themselves to cultivate and convert the resources God has made available to them from potential to tangible assets. Stooping low shows you care. It shows you are willing to empty yourself to create room to absorb the needs of others and transform the demand by the ability in you. If you are too full of yourself, you offload on others, and people generally dislike being a dumping ground. You cannot honestly stoop low without knowing what the reward will be. I once said, "*the Holy Ghost works better when there is a vision broken down into goals.*"

> [24]*[Aroused] by faith Moses, when he had grown to maturity and become great, refused to be called the son of Pharaoh's daughter,* [25]*Because he preferred to share the oppression [suffer the hardships] and bear the shame of the people of God rather than to have the fleeting enjoyment of a sinful life.*
>
> [26]*He considered the contempt and abuse and shame [borne for] the Christ (the Messiah Who was to come) to be greater wealth than all the treasures of Egypt, for he looked forward and away to the reward (recompense).*
>
> Hebrews 11:24-26 (AMP)

Someone might say this is working for personal gain. Well, yes it is. If my gain leaves a trail of people who have activated their potential and are delivering results after the God kind, then it's worth it. The important thing is that gain at the expense of others is wickedness. Gain with others is godly.

One of the motivating factors for writing at the rate I do is the thought of someone out there whose destiny depends on reading a statement from the book or hearing someone replay the revelation they received from the book. You can imagine how I felt when someone told me he started reading the book "The Knowledge of the Hebrew Boys" and after reading the first few pages, he stopped and went to share what he had read with his prayer team. I felt we were succeeding in the goal of changing the world one mind at a time.

An Alignment of Core Values

You can never deploy your full spiritual and mental capacity on something you do not believe in. The greatest salespeople today, sell products they believe in. They meet the specific needs of the client. This shows you are more interested in eliminating the need of the client than you are in making money off them. Every disappointed client is a mind holding you captive by restraining the growth of your business through their testimony.

You need to determine what defines your core values. If your core values do not flow out of your relationship with God, whatever comes out of you will attempt to destroy value in others and contaminate their core values. God will hold you accountable for the contaminated core values you create in others because a tainted core value can send someone to hell.

> *5And whoso shall receive one such little child in my name receiveth me. 6But whoso shall offend one of these little ones which believe in me, it were better for him that a millstone were hanged about his neck, and that he were drowned in the depth of the sea.*
>
> *Matthew 18:5-6*

Who are the little ones but people who do not have the relevant information or the mental capacity to make the judgement call themselves? These are people holding on to God for the performance of His Word and have no alternative. You are to treat such ones as if they were Jesus in need. If you take advantage of their situation, God will speedily avenge them because He is the God of the fatherless and the motherless. He is the parent of the person who is like a child without access to parental guidance.

Your core values should be things you define from the Word of God. They are reasonings and contemplations that are rooted in the Word of God that control your actions. A product or service that does not glorify God can never excite me. If it is not something I can claim to be *"deputising"* for God on, it is not worth my energy. God cannot flow through you, and a product or service that destroys His kingdom flows out of you.

The Result of Work Must Generate Satisfaction

If you perceive that you paid too much for a product or service, you will not be satisfied even if the facts demonstrate otherwise. What is my point? Work must generate satisfaction, and satisfaction cannot exist without expectation. Every time God made anything, in the six days during creation, He was satisfied with what He did. At the end of the six days, He was delighted. The expression of His works met His expectation.

[31]And God saw every thing that he had made, and, behold, it was very good. And the evening and the morning were the sixth day.

Genesis 1:31

Work generates satisfaction at every stage energy is applied. You need to be satisfied at each of these stages to avoid dissatisfaction at the end. God saw "*good*" every day before seeing "*very good*" at the end. If you are dissatisfied about something, express it quickly; do not suppress this dissatisfaction because even if the finished product is good, your dissatisfaction with a component will remain in your consciousness and will hinder your effective use of the product.

When I was younger, I used to drive an old car, and that meant spending a lot of time with road-side mechanics. I did not have the funds or the time to go to a decent garage to get the car fixed. Rather than buying new parts, I just got the mechanic to patch up the fault. This gave the impression that the car was working right and sustained me till the next patch job. However, even though the car was moving, I could not drive the car the way I wanted for fear of being too rough and breaking the patch. In other words, the consciousness of the patch limited my ability to express myself with the tool of the car creatively. The patch probably could have withstood the demands I placed on it, but my consciousness limited me.

See what God says.

[10]For every beast of the forest is mine, and the cattle upon

a thousand hills.

[11]I know all the fowls of the mountains: and the wild beasts of the field are mine.

[12]If I were hungry, I would not tell thee: for the world is mine, and the fulness thereof.

Psalm 50:10-12

Can you imagine if you had in your consciousness, that there are certain conditions under which God will be hungry and require the sort of food we eat? The knowledge of a defective component in a product will affect how you value the finished product. Where the resource is a person, you need the spirit of God to help you deal with the mental perception as you may end up being judgemental, exercising judgement based on what you see.

[16]Do not err, my beloved brethren.

[17]Every good gift and every perfect gift is from above, and cometh down from the Father of lights, with whom is no variableness, neither shadow of turning.

[18]Of his own will begat he us with the word of truth, that we should be a kind of firstfruits of his creatures.

James 1:16-18

Build your expectation for success from the Word of God and make sure you do not settle for less. Every vision from above comes with a provision for delivery. Aim for excellence at whatever level you are at but remember, a lot of people want to *"arrive excellent."* Excellence is not a gift, but the product of a combination of traits that you allow to grow. People with excellent results are diligent, they have great attention to detail, they are not afraid to start over again, and they learn extensively by study and observation. Excellence is not a character trait. It is a work or product trait. However, what determines whether you strive for excellence or not is a mindset you have.

The Number of People Involved

Work is better when you are not on the journey alone. From the story of creation, we see that God did not work as a single personality. There were multiple personalities at work.

> *26And God said, LET US make man in OUR IMAGE, after OUR LIKENESS: and let them have dominion over the fish of the sea, and over the fowl of the air, and over the cattle, and over all the earth, and over every creeping thing that creepeth upon the earth.*
>
> *Genesis 1:26*

> *26God said, Let Us [Father, Son, and Holy Spirit] make mankind in Our image, after Our likeness, and let them have complete authority over the fish of the sea, the birds of the air, the [tame] beasts, and over all of the earth, and over everything that creeps upon the earth.*
>
> *Genesis 1:26 (AMP)*

We know all three personalities were involved in creation, for the Holy Spirit was present in *Genesis 1:2* when the Spirit of God moved over the face of the waters, as was Jesus through who all things were created.

> *3By faith we understand that the worlds [during the successive ages] were framed (fashioned, put in order, and equipped for their intended purpose) by the word of God,*

so that what we see was not made out of things which are visible.

Hebrews 11:3(AMP)

3All things were made and came into existence through Him; and without Him was not even one thing made that has come into being.

John 1:3 (AMP)

There are also numerous examples in scripture where people were engaged in work for God in pairs. I am not saying that God cannot work with individuals. He can, and He does. However, there can only be one visionary. Numerous visionaries on the same work will cause division. While there can be only one visionary, there is room for multiple missionaries. Every profession has ministers. Church-focused missionaries start churches while business-focussed missionaries start businesses. The same signs that manifest in starting and running a church should manifest in starting and running a business. God is as interested in the business as he is in the Church. They are both spiritual. Let us look at some of the pairings in scripture.

Moses and Aaron

14And the anger of the LORD was kindled against Moses, and he said, Is not Aaron the Levite thy brother? I know that he can speak well. And also, behold, he cometh forth to meet thee: and when he seeth thee, he will be glad in his heart.

15And thou shalt speak unto him, and put words in his mouth: and I will be with thy mouth, and with his mouth, and will teach you what ye shall do.

[16]And he shall be thy spokesman unto the people: and he shall be, even he shall be to thee instead of a mouth, and thou shalt be to him instead of God.

Exodus 4:14-16

This is an interesting pair. God's anger did not lead to the pairing of Moses and Aaron. He was angry with Moses' excuses. Aaron was already on his way to meet Moses because God had compensated for Moses' handicap. Many times, people wait to remove handicaps in their lives before embarking on the assignments God has for them but sometimes the compensating strength you require is in another individual called along with you. God could have removed Moses's stammering, but He did not.

Embrace the help God has provided around you. He will deal with the shortcoming as you go. Your trust needs to be in God and not in your ability. God is too big to be limited by your disability. I remember a preacher I knew in Nigeria years ago. This great prophet of God was blind, yet people who had severe sicknesses, including blindness, got healed at his meetings.

Bezaleel and Aholieb

[1]And the LORD spake unto Moses, saying,

[2]See, I have called by name Bezaleel the son of Uri, the son of Hur, of the tribe of Judah:

[3]And I have filled him with the spirit of God, in wisdom, and in understanding, and in knowledge, and in all manner of workmanship, [4]To devise cunning works, to work in gold, and in silver, and in brass, [5]And in cutting of stones, to set them, and in carving of timber, to work in all manner of

workmanship.

⁶And I, behold, I have given with him Aholiab, the son of Ahisamach, of the tribe of Dan: and in the hearts of all that are wise hearted I have put wisdom, that they may make all that I have commanded thee;

Exodus 31:1-6

Bezaleel was called by name but with Bezaleel came Aholiab who was of a completely different tribe. I do not know why God works this way, but He does, and it is something we need to embrace.

In case we thought it was an Old Testament occurrence, these examples in the New Testament still reflect the mind of God on this.

The Seventy

Even Jesus continued by sending people two by two. I believe you need to look around you. There may be someone God has called alongside you or you being called alongside someone else. You may have been struggling with starting your own business, and things have not taken off as you wanted. Seek the face of God, maybe you are called alongside someone else.

¹After these things the LORD appointed other seventy also, and sent them two and two before his face into every city and place, whither he himself would come.

Luke 10:1

Barnabas and Saul

> ¹*Now there were in the church that was at Antioch certain prophets and teachers; as Barnabas, and Simeon that was called Niger, and Lucius of Cyrene, and Manaen, which had been brought up with Herod the tetrarch, and Saul.*
>
> ²*As they ministered to the Lord, and fasted, the Holy Ghost said, Separate me Barnabas and Saul for the work whereunto I have called them.*
>
> ³*And when they had fasted and prayed, and laid their hands on them, they sent them away.*
>
> ⁴*So they, being sent forth by the Holy Ghost, departed unto Seleucia; and from thence they sailed to Cyprus.*
>
> *Acts 13:1-4*

A while ago, a friend and I took our children to dance classes with a group that used the hall of a Methodist Church. While the children were in the dance class, my friend and I played table football when a lady approached us and asked if we lived locally. She said she and her colleagues had been trying to create programs to attract youths to the Church, but for some reason, things were not working out as expected.

I then began to speak to her about the Holy Spirit saying He was the energiser she needed to connect with to make things come alive. While we spoke with her, someone took the ball we were using for the table football game. So I jokingly asked if she could get us a new ball since she worked there. Surprisingly, she had the ball, so I followed her to her office while we continued to talk about the Holy Spirit. I started talking about the book I was working on at that time

"Piercing the Spirit of the Sadducees." **Suddenly, she** said, "that Holy Ghost you are talking about, I want it now!" Now, this response was not what I expected. My mind suddenly went into overdrive, How can you lay hands on someone (*a lady*) in a public place? What if she suddenly claims, I harassed her? I had never met this lady before, how do I know she really wants the Holy Spirit?

At this time, my friend was wondering what was taking time and came to get me. When he realised what was going on and the *"dilemma"* in which I found myself, he said to me, *"Follow your heart."* So I asked her if we could pray somewhere and she pulled open the drawer of her desk and brought out the key to the main church auditorium. So my friend and I and our children, who had now finished their class, went in with her. At this point, the questions in my mind were now about her receiving the baptism. What if she does not get filled? What is she going to think? Thank God He is greater than our minds and He cares because the Holy Spirit had brought a scripture to my mind. *Acts 10:44*, *"While Peter yet spake...the Holy Ghost fell..."*

By now, I was excited because I realised that I did not need to touch her. We then proceeded to take her through two scriptures in Acts of the Apostles, confirmed she had given her life to Jesus and before we could think any further, this wonderful sister just started to flow in tongues glorifying God.

Why did I share this story? Had my friend not been there to encourage me, I may have denied the lady the miracle she so desperately desired. I am not saying you should never do anything alone, but sometimes having someone else there goes a long way.

What was even more fascinating for me was what God spoke to my heart as I drove home. He said, *"You know, the same Holy Ghost that was present to fill that lady is the same Holy Ghost that will be available if she had been in a wheelchair."*

So really, you do not need to be in *"crusade mode"* to see the miraculous. Only believe, and God will surpass your mind.

Glory to God!.

Chapter Key Points

The first revelation we have of God in scriptures is that

of a working God and the products He created

If you are too full of yourself, you offload on others, and people generally dislike being a dumping ground

Highly productive resources are productive on purpose

4

The Principle of Work - II

Work is something we need to get right for it to be effective. If you do not enjoy what you do, you will likely be underperforming at it. High performers enjoy what they do and are creative at finding solutions. They create solutions in problem situations. They find solutions using the same raw materials that others used but failed. Do you know anyone who is highly productive and does not have something they are good at? Your answer is probably "No."

Jesus, for me, is the most productive person to have lived on earth. His impact was so great that it divided time. He left His followers with the ability to replicate His work. Have you ever worked with someone who is highly productive and also knows how to make others as highly productive as themselves? These are the type of people I call HRAs (Human Resource Assets). If we can follow in Jesus' footsteps, maybe we could be as productive as He is. Jesus even talked about us doing greater works than He did.

> [12]*Verily, verily, I say unto you, He that believeth on me, the works that I do shall he do also; and greater works than these shall he do; because I go unto my Father.*
>
> *John 14:12*

I am sure you realise that Jesus gave the highest quality possible so we cannot exceed the quality of the work He did. The "greater works" here, I believe, refers to the opportunity to do more, and even this is quite something because what we have recorded in the bible does not reflect all He did. John said if someone had contemplated writing about all of His works, the world would not contain what they could have written.

> [25]*And there are also many other things which Jesus did, the which, if they should be written every one, I suppose that even the world itself could not contain the books that should be written. Amen.*
>
> *John 21:25*

So the "*greater works*" is quite an expectation that should be motivating us to maximise every single day. Getting work right is not a mystery. Work, like most things, is governed by principles that guarantee a favourable outcome when applied. Genuinely successful people usually apply principles and have thought patterns that unsuccessful people ignore or are ignorant of. Let us look at a few of these principles from stories in the bible.

What Do People Come To You For?

Some years ago, in the church I attended at the time, while our team leader introduced a new team member, she said one or two things about the old members. She chose to highlight what each person did. One was a banker, the other a dentist and so on, but when she got to me, she hesitated and then said something like "business strategist." While we all laughed about the description she gave, I was a little startled because I recognised a severe problem. Whatever it is I was referring to as "work" at that time was not clear to her. What then would others think? Think about the people who are closest to you.

Do you know what their dominant strength is? Your dominant strength is what draws people to you, and your most visible weakness is what keeps them away. What do people come to you for? When they see you, what do they think about? When you see the Queen of England, you do not think about boxing; you most likely think royalty. When you see Barack Obama, you do not think fashion first; you probably think power or something along those lines. When you go to the bank, you are not expecting to see your lawyer or your doctor there to give you financial advice.

Look at the experience this Samaritan lady had with Jesus at the well.

> *27And upon this came his disciples, and marvelled that he talked with the woman: yet no man said, What seekest thou? or, Why talkest thou with her?*
>
> *28The woman then left her waterpot, and went her way into*

the city, and saith to the men,

[29]Come, see a man, which told me all things that ever I did: is not this the Christ?

[30]Then they went out of the city, and came unto him.

John 4:27-30

We can see that Jesus had a great impact on her when we look at the remarks she made in Verse 29, "Come, see a man, which told me all things that ever I did" How would you be described? If the description is too complex, you are most likely a complicated person and potential clients would avoid you. We all want to keep our lives simple. You need to ensure that your dominant strength is undeniable and easily described in simple language. This is crucial because for your clients or customers to refer you, you and your product need to stick in people's minds very quickly.

So, I made a conscious decision to change this. The challenge was how to change. I had a technology background but had moved into management within my sector, so I had no choice but to go to God for help, who had mercy on me and opened my eyes to the importance of capturing my thoughts in written form and creating books out of them. So you can imagine how excited I was when not too long ago, I came across the same team leader long after I had left the team and she asked me how the books were doing. Things had turned around; I now had a dominant identity for that season of my life.

I should say here; your dominant identity may change over time. Be okay with that but leverage the past and don't let it go to waste. If you are someone who has interests in many areas, be recognised by a term that encapsulates what you do in simple language. You could call yourself an entrepreneur or investor or something like that. Jesus made His message simple. He called Himself the saviour of the world. Very successful organisations also do not have any secrecy about them. If you hear the name Oracle and you are in the technology sector, you do not think of an agricultural company; you think computer company. This is the same thing that comes to mind when you think of Microsoft. If you hear Apple, I am sure you almost immediately think of an iPhone, iPad or some other "i" before thinking of the fruit. Why? Apple selling over 100million iPhones worldwide could be a valid response. This does not include the high sales they made on other products. Microsoft's ubiquitous presence on the desktop could also be a valid reason. So, what do people come to you for?

Get Training From the Best

The VisualThesaurus has one of the most explosive translations of the word "*training*" that I have come across. It defines training as "*activity leading to skilled behaviour*" or "*the result of good upbringing (especially knowledge of correct social behaviour)*" Training is about developing skilled behaviour in the application of the principles of life. Training starts from the time a child is born.

Just recently, I visited close relatives I had not seen in a while, and we were catching up on things and talking generally. In the course of the conversation, one of them, who was old enough to be my father said he was surprised at some of the things I was saying because I was very young when those events happened. I told him that children see with the eyes and capture images. They may not be able to process the pictures adequately as children, but as they grow, they will connect the dots and draw conclusions which could reinforce belief systems. It is extremely critical that we expose children to right images even in the years we think they are too young to understand.

> *⁶Train up a child in the way he should go [and in keeping with his individual gift or bent], and when he is old he will not depart from it.*
>
> *Proverbs 22:6 (AMP)*

Training needs to be in the context of the natural gifts and talents of the child. A child trained against their natural talents and gifts is likely to become dysfunctional. Even after the completion of their training, there will be an inner dissatisfaction in what they are doing. Parents and guardians have a responsibility to make sure they get this right.

Jesus, at an early age, knew to seek out the highest level of knowledge possible for his assignment. At the young age of twelve, he could stay in a town alone without His parents in search of relevant knowledge linked to his assignment.

> *⁴⁶After three days they found Him [came upon Him] in the [court of the] temple, sitting among the teachers, listening to them and asking them questions.*

47And all who heard Him were astonished and overwhelmed with bewildered wonder at His intelligence and understanding and His replies.

48And when they [Joseph and Mary] saw Him, they were amazed; and His mother said to Him, Child, why have You treated us like this? Here Your father and I have been anxiously looking for You [distressed and tormented].

49And He said to them, How is it that you had to look for Me? Did you not see and know that it is necessary [as a duty] for Me to be in My Father's house and [occupied] about My Father's business?

50But they did not comprehend what He was saying to them.

Luke 2:46-50 (AMP)

Verse 49 clearly shows that His being in the temple was a necessity for the purpose for which He had to work. So what is the necessary training and development you need for the work you are engaged in? Jesus, the one born directly by God, as a necessity, needed training from well-developed trainers, teachers, and doctors of the law. His young age notwithstanding, He did what was necessary to learn these skills. You can never be too anointed to learn. The task is finding the right trainers to train you. Do whatever is necessary to learn from the right trainer. A little inconvenience goes a long way. Find a trainer with the right level of experience to transfer knowledge and the right spiritual emotions that will help you. Anyone can train, but not everyone can train with the right spirit to effect a change in mindset.

Paul, one of the greatest apostles, was trained by

a teacher called Gamaliel, but who was Gamaliel? There must have been something weighty about the training from Gamaliel for Paul to have referred to him the way he did.

> [3] *I am a Jew, born in Tarsus of Cilicia but reared in this city. At the feet of Gamaliel I was educated according to the strictest care in the Law of our fathers, being ardent [even a zealot] for God, as all of you are today.*
>
> Acts 22:3 (AMP)

Fortunately, there is some information about him in the scriptures. So, let us look at some of the things that made Gamaliel unique. These are things you need to identify when you are looking for your trainer.

> [34] *But a certain Pharisee in the council (Sanhedrin) named Gamaliel, a teacher of the Law, highly esteemed by all the people, standing up, ordered that the apostles be taken outside for a little while.*
>
> [35] *Then he addressed them [the council, saying]: Men of Israel, take care in regard to what you propose to do concerning these men.*
>
> [36] *For before our time there arose Theudas, asserting himself to be a person of importance, with whom a number of men allied themselves, about [400]; but he was killed and all who had listened to and adhered to him were scattered and brought to nothing.*
>
> [37] *And after this one rose up Judas the Galilean, [who led an uprising] during the time of the census, and drew away a popular following after him; he also perished and all his adherents were scattered.*
>
> [38] *Now in the present case let me say to you, stand off (withdraw) from these men and let them alone. For if*

this doctrine or purpose or undertaking or movement is of human origin, it will fail (be overthrown and come to nothing);

[39]But if it is of God, you will not be able to stop or overthrow or destroy them; you might even be found fighting against God!

[40]So, convinced by him, they took his advice; and summoning the apostles, they flogged them and sternly forbade them to speak in or about the name of Jesus, and allowed them to go.

Acts 5:34-40 (AMP)

Gamaliel was a teacher of the law. Teachers break things down into its components and to impart understanding. Some students fail, not because they are bad students but because they had bad teachers. The teacher you listen to can determine the future you live. The knowledge imparted to you by your teachers is what determines the response you have to the issues of life. Good schools are not good schools for nothing. They do something the not so good schools are not doing and avoid some things the not so good schools do.

All people highly esteemed Gamaliel. To have people regard you is something you earn. There is no way Gamaliel could have earned this esteem if what He was living was different from what he was teaching. Do you respect someone who says one thing and does another? Do you respect someone whose counsel has consistently produced bad outcomes for you? Do you regard highly the counsel of someone in an area where they have not demonstrated superior understanding? Will you go to someone who has not successfully built a credible institution to teach you how to build yours? I suspect your answer will be "No" to these questions.

Gamaliel understood that some things have their origin in God while others in men (Verse 39). Anything that comes out of God has a propelling force behind it that no human wisdom or strength can resist. This is why I say effective work is work that has its roots in God. It is the work that the forces of heaven support. It is the will of God in heaven being expressed on earth through the works of our hand. It is the work that requires daily sustenance from God as we look up to Him for mercy while praise rises from our lips to Him. The true source of sustenance for man should be something that proceeds out of the Word of God.

Gamaliel understood the use of case studies. What is one of the things that make some of the leading business schools in the world today, the leading institutions they are? Case Studies. It is said that a typical two year MBA programme from a leading institution may require students to study between six hundred and eight hundred case studies with each having between two and thirty pages.

This is an excerpt of the Harvard Business School MBA program taken from their website (*http://www. hbs.edu/mba/ academics/*) to give you an idea of what I am talking about.

There are special moments that pull everything we have learned into focus. When theory, practice, experience and talent all come to one sharp point — a decision that shapes a definitive course of action.

When it's no longer an issue of what can be done, but of what you will do.

Decisive moments define a Harvard Business School education. Here, everything from Section life to case studies, from field- based learning to international Immersions, culminates in one larger lesson — what it means to assume leadership within an ever-growing, ever-changing world.

Through case method courses, FIELD projects, multimedia simulations, and more, you exercise the leadership skills you will practice in business and beyond. The issues are complex, the stakes high, and the demands challenging. But as a result, you leave HBS with lessons in leadership that are practical, priceless, and most importantly, real.

Why case studies? Life has a way of repeating itself. There is nothing new under the sun. Look at how Gamaliel used case studies.

[35]Then he addressed them [the council, saying]: Men of Israel, take care in regard to what you propose to do concerning these men.

[36]For before our time there arose Theudas, asserting himself to be a person of importance, with whom a number of men allied themselves, about [400]; but he was killed and all who had listened to and adhered to him were scattered and brought to nothing.

[37]And after this one rose up Judas the Galilean, [who led an uprising] during the time of the census, and drew away a popular following after him; he also perished and all his adherents were scattered.

[38]Now in the present case let me say to you…..

Acts 5:35-38 (AMP)

Case studies create patterns in the mind. They create

ready-made images of solutions. I remember hearing the leader of one of the most successful churches in Nigeria saying he studied the biographies of over thirty- five selected ministries, gaining the wisdom of someone almost twice his age before he started in ministry. For the Christian out there trying to make an impact, it takes more than just the anointing to succeed. We can follow patterns to gain wisdom. Paul referred to this when he talked about the training of Gamaliel. Look at the beginning of *verse 38*. All Gamaliel was saying was "I have seen this pattern before" and I know what the solution should be. The method worked because *verse 40* tells us the result.

> *40So, convinced by him, they took his advice;*
>
> *Acts 5:40*

Is your trainer using case studies? Have they studied multiple situations and seen different perspectives? Who is the greatest custodian of case studies you can go to for training? Well, we could start with the One who has been around the longest, who has personally witnessed and been involved in orchestrating things, the One whose very name is Wisdom, who is a master on all subjects past, present and future. He is the power of the Ancient of Days.

The Holy Spirit should be your first and ultimate teacher. His teachings are flawless. He uses everything around you to show you patterns. Remember, *"Go to the ant, thou sluggard"* in *Proverbs 6:6*. Moreover, He has inside knowledge of all situations at all times. What is even more exciting is that He is always with you. You cannot go anywhere that He will not be able to reach you.

Understand Yourself – What Is Written In the Book Concerning You?

The starting point for effectiveness at work is gaining a full understanding of yourself. You cannot deliver value beyond what you believe of yourself. Finding out about you could involve doing a bit of research; find out what happened when you were young? What were the prevailing circumstances? Were there any pointers you missed? There is a great story in every person's childhood, no matter how dark or bleak it may have been. If you look closely enough, there is something to be proud of.

> *5Wherefore when he cometh into the world, he saith, Sacrifice and offering thou wouldest not, but a body hast thou prepared me:*
>
> *6In burnt offerings and sacrifices for sin thou hast had no pleasure. 7Then said I, Lo, I come (in the volume of the book it is written of me,) to do thy will, O God.*
>
> *8Above when he said, Sacrifice and offering and burnt offerings and offering for sin thou wouldest not, neither hadst pleasure therein; which are offered by the law;*
>
> *9Then said he, Lo, I come to do thy will, O God. He taketh away the first, that he may establish the second.*
>
> *10By the which will we are sanctified through the offering of the body of Jesus Christ once for all.*
>
> *Hebrews 10:5-10*

Jesus found the place *(Isaiah 61:1-3)* where the book said something about Him. So if Jesus, our role model, looked in "The Book" to find what was written about Him, maybe looking in "The Book" is an excellent place to find what is written about you. Many of us have had experiences that shape our very being. Memories of childhood experiences form patterns in the mind which in turn shape our belief systems. The good news is that while we cannot change the facts about these situations, we can change the way we feel about them. We can see them as stepping stones to the dreams we desire. Jesus did not see the cross as an end; He saw it as a path through which His resurrection power was going to flow to humanity. Where are you looking for what has been written about you? "The Book" contains something for everybody, and all we have to do is believe what it says.

Jesus is not the only one who found something in "The Book." John the Baptist was *the voice of the one crying in the wilderness.*" John Alexander Dowie found *How God anointed Jesus Christ of Nazareth with the Holy Ghost and Power..."* in Acts 10:38. Kenneth E. Hagin found faith in Mark 11:22-24, Smith Wigglesworth found in Mark 9:23 that *All things are possible to him who believes,*" I saw in Isaiah 51:16 that *God has put His words in my mouth and covered me in the shadow of His hands.*" What have you discovered about yourself?

As you prayerfully study the Word of God, The Holy Spirit will reveal what is written in "The Book" concerning your life. In "The Book" you will come across the instructions and patterns that will come alive for you and you will pick up the voice of God speaking directly to you. When you know what is written about you and you are convinced about it, it burns like a fire in you and propels you to greater heights effortlessly. I have never met an underperformer who believes strongly in themselves, and I have never met a high performer who does not believe in themselves.

Finding what is written about you will determine where you can draw strength from. Understand what you are good at right now and what you need to develop but use "The Book" to determine your limitations.

Give Every Customer the Same Quality Service

Do not judge your client by their outward appearance. Wealthy people do not always look wealthy. The woman at the well certainly did not look like someone who could have had such influence to get the other men to come to the well based on the message, *"Come, see a man, which told me all things that ever I did."*

There are a few things about this woman we need to take into consideration. Going through a separation or divorce from a husband or wife is a very emotionally draining experience. This woman had not been through one or two but five, so she must have been emotionally shattered.

> *16Jesus saith unto her, Go, call thy husband, and come hither.*
>
> *17The woman answered and said, I have no husband. Jesus said unto her, Thou hast well said, I have no husband:*
>
> *18For thou hast had five husbands; and he whom thou now*

hast is not thy husband: in that saidst thou truly.

John 4:16-18

Despite the breakdown of the previous marriages, she was still willing to work on marriage and build a new one. A lot of times, not so good experiences represent a reason clients switch providers.

Good clients sometimes come disguised, and quality service generates repeat business. I remember the story of a friend who had used a particular agent to acquire a piece of property and was very satisfied with the work of the agent. Ten years later, when he needed the same service, he went to look for the agent that had helped him ten years earlier.

Think about the service or product you call work. If you were on the receiving end of these, would you come back for more? Do not judge yourself based on your intentions or potential; judge yourself based on facts. Did the last sale create the intended outcome for the client? When they opened the package you delivered, were they excited or disappointed? Would they be willing to refer you? Not only was this woman willing to refer Jesus, but she was also so satisfied that her referrals were immediate.

Study your customers, and keep the ones that are not draining your energy and resources but even when you innovate, maintain the same quality product or service. If the taste of McDonald fries is different between franchises, you may question if you visited a McDonald franchise. This sort of experience does nothing but create doubt in the mind of your customers. Look at what the men said when they came and experienced Jesus personally:

> [39]And many of the Samaritans of that city believed on him for the saying of the woman, which testified, He told me all that ever I did. [40]So when the Samaritans were come unto him, they besought him that he would tarry with them: and he abode there two days.
>
> [41]And many more believed because of his own word;
>
> [42]And said unto the woman, Now we believe, not because of thy saying: for we have heard him ourselves, and know that this is indeed the Christ, the Saviour of the world.

John 4:39-42

They believed not just because of the words of the woman, they believed because of their own experience. Strive to create the same experience for all your clients. People define you by the experience you create for them. Bad companies are those that have given bad experiences to enough clients till the message goes around that the service from the company is terrible. What do you do when you get a good deal on something you buy? You will most likely tell others. Manage quality right if you want to enjoy the benefits of work.

Chapter Key Points

Do you know anyone who is highly productive and does not have something they are good at?

Genuinely successful people usually apply principles and have thought patterns that unsuccessful people ignore or are ignorant of

You need to ensure that your dominant strength is undeniable and easily described in simple language

Good schools are not good schools for nothing. They do something the not so good schools are not doing and avoid some things the not so good schools do

5

Principle of Work -III

*T*here is a desire in most people to want to make a difference in life. We all want to live a life that will make an impact. Many things influence what and where to exert our spiritual, emotional and physical energy. Unfortunately, some of our experiences are not particularly good ones, and sometimes the outflow of this energy could have destructive tendencies to both the individual and humanity if not appropriately channelled.

Our inner motivations usually drive our actions. Inner fears of loss and ability to recreate could cause someone to hoard things and live in penury all their lives only to die, and we discover a secret store of valuables. Others give away their wealth to help others avoid the poverty they experienced in their childhood. This inner motivation, whatever it is, is the catalyst for real work.

The Spirit or the Soul

Not many people will argue against the fact that we as humans have a soul. If you are a believer in Jesus, you go a step further and believe that the real person is a spirit which is made alive through the confession of Jesus Christ as Lord and Saviour. Looking through the Bible, we discover that truly a spirit exists which is very distinct from the soul.

> [23]And the very God of peace sanctify you wholly; and I pray God your whole spirit and soul and body be preserved blameless unto the coming of our Lord Jesus Christ.
>
> 1 Thessalonians 5:23

We are starting to see a robust scientific correlation between the soul, the body and the state of the spirit. The spirit is the anchor that holds the soul and the body together. The right consciousness of the spirit can produce supernatural effects on the body and make the body behave in a certain way when confronted with deep adversity.

> [14]The spirit of a man will sustain his infirmity; but a wounded spirit who can bear?
>
> Proverbs 18:14

> [14]The strong spirit of a man sustains him in bodily pain or trouble, but a weak and broken spirit who can raise up or bear?
>
> Proverbs 18:14 (AMP)

So everyone is a spirit which is the real person but since there is no separate activity to introduce this spirit into us, I believe, we can conclude the person is born with a spirit. The question then is this. Where does this spirit come from? Well, there is only one Father of spirits, and that is God. He is a Spirit (*John 4:24*) and the only Spirit that gives birth to spirits.

9Furthermore we have had fathers of our flesh which corrected us, and we gave them reverence: shall we not much rather be in subjection unto the Father of spirits, and live?

Hebrews 12:9

So, for every child to have a spirit, the only place that spirit could have come from is God. I also believe this would hold irrespective of the person to whom the child is born. Therefore, every child born is on an assignment from heaven.

So what is the importance of this spirit and soul distinction, and how is it related to work? I believe real work comes from the spirit and not the soul, and the most potent form of work is when the expression of it is rooted in the Father of spirits. God in heaven has a will and will do what is required to establish His will on earth. So any work you are engaged in that advances the will of God will receive the backing of Heaven, whether you are a believer or not. For example, Jesus, before the foundation of the world, died for us while we were sinners, and we did not do anything to earn or influence that love that He had for us.

If God could use an ass (*Numbers 22:23-31*) to have an intelligent conversation with a prophet, He can use anything, even stones. (*Luke 19:35-41*). Almost everything in the prophetic agenda of God will find expression whether there is a believer present or not.

Some will even be able to cast out devils in His name but not make Heaven. You make heaven based on a conscious decision to accept Jesus as Lord and Saviour and not because of the works you do or the works done through you. Never mistake the supernatural to be confirmation of a right relationship with God. God, despite your shortcomings, may allow things to happen, to a level, for the benefit of bringing answered prayers to His children.

The Composition of Work

So what exactly should work consist of? I think the easiest way to answer this is to look at what Jesus came to do and what He called His assignment in Luke 4:17-20. For me, I had read these verses many times and focused on one particular line of thought that "Jesus was anointed." Sometimes we believers are guilty of being so "spiritual" to the degree that we miss pertinent truth from the Word of God. Yes, Jesus was anointed, but what was He anointed to do? What group was He to reach out to?

> *[17]And there was delivered unto him the book of the prophet Esaias. And when he had opened the book, he found the place where it was written,*

> *[18]The Spirit of the Lord is upon me, because he hath anointed me to preach the gospel to the poor; he hath sent me to heal the brokenhearted, to preach deliverance to the captives, and recovering of sight to the blind, to set at liberty them that are bruised,*

> *[19]To preach the acceptable year of the Lord.*

> *[20]And he closed the book, and he gave it again to the minister, and sat down. And the eyes of all them that were*

Luke 4:17-20

Let me share a perspective of this assignment of Jesus because it encapsulates what work for a believer should include. Jesus' work addressed specific groups, and He did different things with each group.

Jesus was anointed for the poor, the brokenhearted, the captives, the blind and the bruised. What? Why such groups? Did He not have advisers to tell Him that these people are "losers" in the game of life and nothing good can come out of them? Thoughts like these are the very ones that lock people out of greatness. Too many people look to expend their spiritual, emotional and physical energies where the person or organisation they are working for represents an outward benefit to them. They have a taker's mentality rather than a giver's one. So when looking for jobs, we ask about remuneration before considering what value we will be to the organisation. Organisations hire value, not cost.

Most organisations and individuals are not happy with cost but will pay a premium for good value. Value is not always apparent, and only skilful scouts know how to discover good value when it comes unpolished. Good value is usually the result of a process.

Have you despised these groups? Have you been too proud to associate with such? Are you part of the group and are too proud to cry for help? Remember, every spirit comes from God and everyone you come across represents potential. Many miss out on enriching opportunities because they inaccurately judge the raw material. Look at the composition of the four hundred men, David, the king of Israel, started with.

> [1]David therefore departed thence, and escaped to the cave Adullam: and when his brethren and all his father's house heard it, they went down thither to him.
>
> [2]And every one that was in distress, and every one that was in debt, and every one that was discontented, gathered themselves unto him; and he became a captain over them: and there were with him about four hundred men.
>
> *1 Samuel 22:1-2*

What I am saying is very simple; make sure the expending of your energy targets these groups. When computers originally came out, they only targeted the rich, maybe not intentionally, but that was the nature of the product at the time. Very few could afford it. The computing industry, until the advent of the personal computer, did not start to explode into the mass market and even further now with mobile devices. Every new cycle of technology has lowered the entry point and opened up significant markets in the process.

When God started His relationship with a people, He began with the Jews, worship had to be at a particular location, it had to happen in Jerusalem but how did Christianity gain the following it has today? God through Jesus opened up the relationship with Him to everyone who believed, effectively lowering the entry point without devaluing the substance.

This concept of targeting "the masses" is an old one

that works and is godly. How was music sold in the past? As early as I can relate with, it was records, tapes, CD, and then things went digital. I'm sure you understand the point now. Ask God for wisdom on how to take what you are doing to these groups of people, and He will surely answer. Follow God's pattern. Remember what I said earlier, think global but start local.

Let us look at the groups Jesus targeted in a little more detail.

The Poor

18The Spirit of the Lord is upon me, because He hath anointed me to preach the gospel to the poor; he hath sent me to heal the brokenhearted, to preach deliverance to the captives, and recovering of sight to the blind, to set at liberty them that are bruised,

Luke 4:18

The poor is a category always associated with lack of financial means but being poor extends beyond this to those who, sometimes for reasons they have no control over, do not have the means (spiritual, mental, financial, emotional) to acquire the necessities of life. These include people who have fallen from the intended purpose of God and cannot get up on their own. These are people who have been overcome by the challenges of life. These include the fatherless and the motherless, the ones who have had severed the normal channels of sustenance.

You may think such dire levels of poverty are not around you because you live in a "developed" economy. Still, the rich, high net-worth individuals are always a minority in any society. The appearance of riches does not guarantee the presence of wealth. What most people call riches may be credit masked as wealth.

Be careful not to confuse access to credit with wealth as such confusion could be very costly both emotionally and physically. Credit is a means, but wealth is a product. Credit is a means that allows the rich to get richer and, in a lot of cases, the poor get poorer. The person with credit is a captive while the one with wealth is a deliverer.

The greatest need of the poor is good news. The news that you can acquire products and services at an affordable price. The news that those things you could only dream about are now affordable and within reach. You can walk into those things you only dreamt of. You now have the license to dream. There is something in the bible called the Lord's release.

[1]*At the end of every seven years thou shalt make a release.*

[2]*And this is the manner of the release: Every creditor that lendeth ought unto his neighbour shall release it; he shall not exact it of his neighbour, or of his brother; because it is called the LORD's release.*

³Of a foreigner thou mayest exact it again: but that which is thine with thy brother thine hand shall release;

Deuteronomy 15:1-3

The gospel is the proclamation of the Lord's release. What is the good news you are bringing to the poor around you? Are you sharing the good news or concurring with every negative and evil report out there? What have people done to you that you have not let go? This is the year of release. Let it go. There is a reward that comes from God for letting things go. He blesses the work of your hand to the degree you let others go.

⁹Beware that there be not a thought in thy wicked heart, saying, The seventh year, the year of release, is at hand; and thine eye be evil against thy poor brother, and thou givest him nought; and he cry unto the LORD against thee, and it be sin unto thee.

¹⁰Thou shalt surely give him, and thine heart shall not be grieved when thou givest unto him: because that for this thing the LORD thy God shall bless thee in all thy works, and in all that thou puttest thine hand unto.

Deuteronomy 15:9-10

What have you done for people who have ideas and have not been able to do anything with it due to one limitation or the other? Act now. Share the good news.

The Broken-hearted

¹⁸The Spirit of the Lord is upon me, because he hath anointed me to preach the gospel to the poor; He hath sent me to heal the brokenhearted, to preach deliverance to the captives, and recovering of sight to the blind, to set at liberty them that are bruised,

Luke 4:18

Disappointment can be very devastating. Some people never recover because some pain is so deep that coherent thinking near impossible.

Recently, I heard the story of a bride whose husband decided not to show up for the wedding. I am sure you can imagine the pain in the heart of that bride, the mixed emotions that would have been looking for answers to the "why me?" question. Is it the husband or the wife who has to deal with infidelity or the child that wonders why they were abused sexually by a parent? Whatever the source, the pain is real.

We also need to remember that it only takes one broken employee multiplied over to have a broken organisation. A broken heart, if not dealt with properly, will affect the sense of judgement a person exhibits. Many people judge situations based on experience and not on facts. A daughter broken by a father can grow up to be a wife that breaks her loving husband and a son broken by a father can be dangerous to a loving wife.

Broken hearts do not always come from things outside your control. Whichever way it comes, broken people need healing. You may be broken-hearted because you ignored signs and warnings along the way, but it does not matter to Jesus. He is a God of mercy and will be merciful. He is familiar with the feelings of rejection, disappointment and failure. He can bring the broken pieces together again. I remember that old nursery rhyme that talks about Humpty Dumpty which says:

1*Humpty Dumpty sate on a wall,*

Humpti Dumpti had a great fall;

Threescore men and threescore more, Cannot place Humpty dumpty as he was before.

And more recently

2*Humpty Dumpty sate on a wall, Humpty Dumpty had a great fall;*

All the king's horses and all the king's men Couldn't put Humpty together again.

Whichever version of the rhyme you take and no matter how broken the pieces, the King of Kings Himself can put you together. Jesus knows what it means to be heartbroken. He came to His own, and His own received Him not. He was of no honour in His own

1 *Joseph Ritson Gammer Gurton's Garland: or, the Nursery Parnassus; a Choice Collection of Pretty Songs and Verses, for the Amusement of All Little Good Children Who Can Neither Read Nor Run (London: Hard- ing and Wright, 1810), p. 36.*
2 *The Oxford Dictionary of Nursery Rhymes (Oxford: Oxford University Press, 1951, 2nd edn., 1997), ISBN 0-19-869111-4, pp. 213-5*

country. Though without sin, He was rejected and bruised by His own for their iniquity. A person you know is more likely to be a source of rejection and heart-ache, so do not be overly concerned when these situations present themselves. Though this requires a conscious effort on the part of the broken, you can certainly overcome the pain.

What are you doing to help troubled organisations get on their feet again? Remember, people make up organisations. The mindset allowed to prevail determines organisational culture. Very few people, if any, can make wise decisions in a broken state. Your energy could help restore confidence. Their products and services could be recast and made more relevant, helping to grow sales and stop the next round of downsizing.

The Captives

[18]The Spirit of the Lord is upon me, because he hath anointed me to preach the gospel to the poor; he hath sent me to heal the brokenhearted, to preach deliverance to the captives, and recovering of sight to the blind, to set at liberty them that are bruised,

Luke 4:18

Captivity is an interesting concept, and it is not a word used very often. "Prisoner of War" is the closest thing I can think of right now. For most people in the world, this is a foreign concept. Not many of us have been in real war situations where a stronger nation overruns the weaker one and takes the people of the weaker nation as prisoners, but a bad experience can imprison the mind. If there is something in you that you want to do like start a business, write a book, develop a new computer software or just go on a holiday and you have not been able to do it because of some obstacles here and there then are you not a captive of these hindrances? What good can happen when we take all excuses out of the way. Many good ideas will come to pass and make the world a better place.

Captives need deliverance from a deliverer that is stronger than their captor. The only way to break free from captivity is through the exercise of strength. No captor lets its captive go without a fight.

[21] When a strong man armed keepeth his palace, his goods are in peace:

[22] But when a stronger than he shall come upon him, and overcome him, he taketh from him all his armour wherein he trusted, and divideth his spoils.

Luke 11:21-22

Captivity is evidence that you have lost a battle. You cannot be a captive without being overrun by a captor. So since you cannot deliver a captive if you are not stronger than their captor, how do you deliver someone from mental captivity?

Firstly, you need to build and develop yourself until you are stronger than the captor or develop an alliance that will give you the necessary muscle to overcome the captor. This is usually one of the critical drivers for mergers and acquisitions. Merge with another company to gain the required strength to take market share. For the believer, this first alliance should be with God because He is above all and stronger than all. He is light, and darkness cannot resist Him. You cannot put on the lights in a dark room, and the darkness decides it does not feel like leaving. This is just not possible. The intensity and direction of light determine how far you can push back the darkness.

Secondly, the captive must have a willingness to accept the change you represent. I am sure that there are many proposals with recommendations that can take organisations to the next level that are still in some executive's email inbox and may never see the light of day. Mental incapacitation does not change because of the availability of knowledge, it changes when wills are changed, decisions made, and actions taken. Most people know what to do to be free; they just never do it. This is why deliverance that does not affect the spirit and the soul is artificial, but the Word of God can go deep into a person to effect a change. Look at these three translations that drive home the point.

12For the Word that God speaks is alive and full of power [making it active, operative, energizing, and effective]; it is sharper than any two-edged sword, penetrating to the dividing line of the breath of life (soul) and [the immortal] spirit, and of joints and marrow [of the deepest parts of our nature], exposing and sifting and analyzing and judging the very thoughts and purposes of the heart.

Hebrews 4:12 (AMP)

12-13God means what he says. What he says goes. His powerful Word is sharp as a surgeon's scalpel, cutting through everything, whether doubt or defense, laying us open to listen and obey. Nothing and no one is impervious to God's Word. We can't get away from it—no matter what.

Hebrews 4:12 (MSG)

11-13 Let us then be eager to know this rest for ourselves, and let us beware that no one misses it through falling into the same kind of unbelief as those we have mentioned. For the Word that God speaks is alive and active; it cuts more keenly than any two-edged sword: it strikes through to the place where soul and spirit meet, to the innermost intimacies of a man's being: it exposes the very thoughts and motives of a man's heart. No creature has any cover from the sight of God; everything lies naked and exposed before the eyes of him with whom we have to do.

Hebrews 4:11-13 (JBP)

Do not remain a captive to whatever has held you captive. Set yourself free by the Word of God then go after other captives to have the exhilarating feeling of setting someone else free. Leave that one more customer with a happy smile on their face.

The Blind

¹⁸The Spirit of the Lord is upon me, because he hath anointed me to preach the gospel to the poor; he hath sent me to heal the brokenhearted, to preach deliverance to the captives, and recovering of sight to the blind, to set at liberty them that are bruised,

Luke 4:18

Blindness usually describes people with reduced functionality in the eyes. Jesus directly addressed this on numerous occasions by physically healing the defective organ of the eye. The bible documents stories on blind people that Jesus healed. In *Matthew 9:27- 30*, He healed two men that followed him. In *Matthew 12:22*, a blind man possessed with a devil was healed. Also, in *Matthew 15:29-31*, Jesus healed the blind that came to him.

All these people were healed of their physical blindness indicating that those who are physically blind are not only important to God, but He can do something about it.

There is something else about blindness that is even more critical. Some scholars say up to eighty per cent of the information intake for an individual comes from the eyes. This means that diminished functionality in the eyes will directly impact your information intake and will leave you mentally weak unless you do something to compensate for this information loss. What is even more fascinating is the fact that the eyes only capture images and stores them in memory, the brain. How we respond to these images depends on other factors outside the control of the eyes.

I remember watching a documentary not too long ago showing how, through technological advancements, medical scientists were attempting to use electronic devices to capture images and send these images to the brain but bypassing the eyes. If successful, then many physically blind people will get scientific help to capture images of their surroundings and live a near-normal life.

Before we look at this crucial task of recovery of sight to the blind, there are a few essential points we cannot overlook. Firstly, we have two eyes in front of the head, and we can only look in one direction at any time. You cannot look forward and look backwards at the same time. If your eyes are open to one area, then they are closed to the other and the direction to which they are open, determines the boundaries of images they can capture.

You cannot be looking forward and have the eyes capture images behind you. So what happened to Adam and Eve in the Bible? We will come back to this story, but I think it is important you read it here.

⁶And when the woman saw that the tree was good for food,

and that it was pleasant to the eyes, and a tree to be desired to make one wise, she took of the fruit thereof, and did eat, and gave also unto her husband with her; and he did eat.

⁷And the eyes of them both were opened, and they knew that they were naked; and they sewed fig leaves together, and made themselves aprons.

Genesis 3:6-7

Secondly, we have two eyes which, when used together, gives a better depth of perception. What you perceive is unique in interpretation, depends on your current location, and is influenced by your past experiences. So you look at an image and see a particular silhouette. Then someone gives you additional information, another perspective, about the image, you look again, and you see something slightly different. Did the image change? No. You had additional information which allowed you to draw different conclusions from the same image. So, to a degree perception is determined by knowledge.

Thirdly, no matter how good your eyesight, your eyes will not function without light. You can look, but you will not see anything. Light allows the eyes to capture the right perspective of the environment, so the brighter the light, the better the perspective.

Reread *Genesis 3:7. "The eyes of them both were opened."* So, if their eyes were now open, they must have been closed for them to have opened. Remember, since your eyes cannot see two places at the same time, whatever their eyes were previously open to, they were now closed to. The source of images captured had changed, and they became blind to what God wanted them to see. The information they received from the devil changed their images and made them blind to God. Their location also changed, which means their perspective would have changed as you cannot have the same perspective from two different locations. Finally, God pushed them out of their location, making it impossible for them to continue to see the right perspective of God. See what Jesus said.

> *39And Jesus said, For judgment I am come into this world, that they which see not might see; and that they which see might be made blind.*
>
> *40And some of the Pharisees which were with him heard these words, and said unto him, Are we blind also?*
>
> *41Jesus said unto them, If ye were blind, ye should have no sin: but now ye say, We see; therefore your sin remaineth.*
>
> *John 9:39-41*

Verse 39 then becomes easy to understand, and the assignment makes sense. The sin of Adam and Eve created the path to a set of images based on death, but Jesus has come to change the images we see.

What introduced the new images Adam and Eve were seeing? Sin. There is nakedness around you that you only become aware of when you grant sin access into our lives. As long as you see images contrary to God, sin is present, and without looking to God, this sin remains.

> *25But whoso looketh into the perfect law of liberty, and continueth therein, he being not a forgetful hearer, but a doer of the work, this man shall be blessed in his deed.*
>
> *James 1:25*

⁸This book of the law shall not depart out of thy mouth; but thou shalt meditate therein day and night, that thou mayest observe to do according to all that is written therein: for then thou shalt make thy way prosperous, and then thou shalt have good success.

Joshua 1:8

So the questions to answer include what images are you putting before the people you interact with? Do people leave you feeling naked, or do they leave you feeling clothed? Are you changing mindsets? Are you introducing light into your environment?

This blindness is the same reason organisations spend millions of dollars on external consultants. They want light in their organisations. They want information that changes their perspective from one of "we need to adapt" to one of *"we have re-aligned, and we know the way forward with this strategic roadmap. We are marching ahead and taking market share."*

Many people are groping in darkness, waiting for your light. Go and preach recovery of sight. Every employee, organisation and industry requires your light for we are now the light of the world.

The Bruised

¹⁸The Spirit of the Lord is upon me, because he hath anointed me to preach the gospel to the poor; he hath sent me to heal the brokenhearted, to preach deliverance to the captives, and recovering of sight to the blind, to set at liberty them that are bruised,

Luke 4:18

Being bruised is very different from being broken. The VisualThesaurus calls a bruise *"an injury that doesn't break the skin but results in some discolouration"* Bruised people need to be set at liberty and not necessarily healed. Jesus was to set at *"liberty"* these bruised ones.

The word *"liberty"* was translated from a greek word which means forgiveness, liberty or remission. Bruised people are people who have suffered some form of reputational damage. These are people being held captive because of the debt they owed society, which they may have paid, but society is refusing to let go. Every time they try to make progress, shortcomings of the past are brought up and cripple them.

The world has a way of bringing up past failures and judging the present with this knowledge. God, on the other hand, has a way of bringing up future possibilities and giving grace in the present to move towards this future.

I remember once I was with a group of prominent sisters who were involved in media. While we sat in the meeting room awaiting the person they had come to see, we were watching the TV when the images of a very prominent actress acting a scene that was not necessarily one we would endorse came up in a commercial. One of the ladies then said something like "Hmm, and she is now a pastor's wife. I wonder what her church members will think when they see these scenes." I thought for a moment and then highlighted the fact that the actress had not had an experience with Jesus at the time she did those scenes. Furthermore, should your past invalidate your present, when true transformation has taken place? Should the fact that you did something wrong yesterday mean you cannot have wise counsel today? We all, most certainly, will have a past we are not too proud of because there was a time we walked with blinded minds.

How does this bruising affect the organisation? You only need to read some newspapers and particularly the tiny, almost hidden sections, where media organisations retract incorrect information to understand the gravity of things. Words are like broken eggs; once spoken, you cannot put things together again.

Imagine a situation where a mistake from a downstream supplier turns into a PR nightmare. Would you stop trading with that supplier even after they have rectified the issue and demonstrated it was an anomaly and not the norm? There are many bruised people around who want to go back into employment but cannot because they made a mistake in their previous company. Still, sometimes, some people need a prison experience of life to change how they think. For example, calls to help ex-convicts may be difficult; it is nevertheless a call we can make. People change in prison. Let us preach liberty to these bruised ones.

The Acceptable Year of the Lord

[19] To preach the acceptable year of the Lord.

[20] And he closed the book, and he gave it again to the minister, and sat down. And the eyes of all them that were in the synagogue were fastened on him.

Luke 4:19-20

I am sure you must have noticed that the message of the acceptable year of the Lord was not to any particular group like the previous ones. One of the most significant emotional challenges people face is gaining acceptance from other people.

Companies spend millions of dollars on market research to find out if the market will accept their products. The young guy wishing to date a girl wonders if his date will take him. The father wonders if his long lost children will accept him back. The children wonder if they will get that seal of approval from their parents, those magical words that say "Well done, I'm proud of you."

Have you ever submitted a proposal that got rejected? In most cases, rejected proposals are not always all wrong. There was likely a portion that did not entirely address the need as much as the client anticipated. But why do we all seek this acceptance?

Acceptance is a sign of approval. It lets you know that a mind is satisfied with the output of your labour. Most people have specific criteria they tick before approving. Acceptance and Approval are profound concepts. The approval gives you confidence and is the foundation on which you build relationships. Acceptance is about you while approval is about your product, but it is challenging to dissociate a person from their product. Your product usually has marks of your personality. Look at a story about Cain and Abel in the book of Genesis.

³And in process of time it came to pass, that Cain brought of the fruit of the ground an offering unto the LORD.

⁴And Abel, he also brought of the firstlings of his flock and of the fat thereof. And the LORD had respect unto Abel and to his offering: ⁵But unto Cain and to his offering he had not respect. And Cain was very wroth, and his countenance fell.

⁶And the LORD said unto Cain, Why art thou wroth? and why is thy countenance fallen?

⁷If thou doest well, shalt thou not be accepted? and if thou doest not well, sin lieth at the door. And unto thee shall be his desire, and thou shalt rule over him.

Genesis 4:3-7

Neither Cain or his offering - the product - got God's approval. We are all unique, and our personality flows through our creation. Never let anyone put this uniqueness down. We are operating under a dispensation where this uniqueness is acceptable to God. Let your work reflect the best possible outcome you can deliver and develop a consciousness that this outcome is an offering going to God. Treat every client's work like a deliverable that God is going to sign off.

What does Jesus do once He finishes talking about acceptance? He closes the book. I believe if you follow the concepts we have talked about in this chapter, you will obtain endorsement and approval from God and will enter into your rest concerning work. You will get to the point where your products and outcomes appear as though the breath of God is carrying them.

Remember, work is godly whether in Church or not. God worked, so be like God and work.

Chapter Key Points

Real work comes from the spirit and not the soul and the most potent form of work is when the expression of it is rooted in the Father of spirits

You make heaven based on a conscious decision to accept Jesus as Lord and Saviour and not because of the works you do or the works that are done through you

A daughter broken by a father can grow up to be a wife that breaks her loving husband and a son broken by a father can be dangerous to a loving wife

Credit is a means, but wealth is a product

6

Working the Talk

I have been in too many meetings where someone brings up a good idea about how to progress a goal and everyone echoes support. We talk about how the concept represents the right course of action for the organisation. Then comes the magic moment when we need to find owners for tasks, and suddenly things change. Everyone is extremely busy and need to check diaries for availability, and the level of creativity expressed in producing excuses is almost miraculous. I'm sure some of you can relate to this situation.

A lot of great ideas end their journey of becoming a reality at this stage simply because there are more talkers than are workers. This is not the case in all places, but it is undoubtedly very prevalent. I have yet to find anyone who achieved success by principles, that does not subscribe to hard work. All are people who exert energy spiritually, mentally and physically. This exertion that I talk about here does not have to be overbearing. Most failed projects do not fail in the big things, they fail in simple things, but simple issues not handled well become greater problems. It is the little foxes that spoil the vine and destroy the tender grapes.

Why do we have more talkers than workers? Well, I believe a lot of people talk without thinking but working without thought is more complicated. I have been in conversations with people on numerous occasions where I have let them speak, and then suddenly they stop and say what they are saying does not make sense. What has happened here is that the mouth went before the mind. Some people are forgiving, and they will give you another chance before they label you as someone who talks without thinking.

For a lot of people, work is a drain. Not many people enjoy what they do. They do what they do for the money to pay the bills and keep them going. They don't pay as much attention to the cause for the work or the vision motivating the action. The "*Thank God, It's Friday*" syndrome, I can't wait to get out of this misery for the next few days.

What we possess is evidence of past work. So, when making decisions, many people think about what they will lose before thinking about what they will gain. What we possess shows how productive our time in the past has been, and we guard this jealously. This is why when you see a product or service, you typically ask how much it costs before fully processing the question of what value you can derive from it. Thinking cost first destroys creativity, but thinking of value first triggers creativity.

We worked with an author that had an exciting funding story. According to her, she suddenly realised she had two laptops and decided to sell one. The buyer, at that point, did not even pay the full price, he only paid a deposit which this author used to pay the deposit on the book. She so desperately wanted the book published. The value proposition had finally overtaken the cost proposition. Interestingly, by the time she got to us, we had an offer going which made the service she wanted even more affordable. We published her book about a year ago.

If you can make this spiritual and mental transition and exert yourself with the Word of God, you will find that there is something you already have that is enough for the next step. It may not be enough for the whole journey, but it is enough for the next step. In the issues of life, you cannot jump seasons. A boy is a boy no matter how tall he is and a girl is a girl no matter how well developed the vital statistics.

You cannot become a professional without being a protégé. What is my point here? If the cost of the next step weighs you down mentally, it is a pointer to the fact that your inner man has not fully comprehended the value for which you want to act.

Workers are progressive people and always have intermediate products to show. Talkers, on the other hand, are usually stagnant and stagnant pools stink. They know everything wrong with everyone and everything, yet they never take action to fix anything.

Let us look at the example God shows us on how to work the talk.

Work Requires Light

God did not start working without light. It was the first thing He created on Day 1 of creation. What is fascinating here is the fact that the light created on Day 1 is different from the light created on Day 4, which gives us the day and night.

> [3]And God said, Let there be light: and there was light.
>
> [4]And God saw the light, that it was good: and God divided the light from the darkness.
>
> [5]And God called the light Day, and the darkness he called Night. And the evening and the morning were the first day.
>
> *Genesis 1:3-5*

God divided the light from darkness on Day 1. The light He called Day and the darkness He called Night. This is the element I refer to as spiritual exertion. If you are going to be a generator of wise counsel and not just a consumer, you will have to learn to separate light from darkness using the Word of God because you cannot work as productively as God requires without this light.

As Christians, we should not work at Night; we should work while it is Day. The entrance of light is the trigger point for motion.

> [3]Jesus answered, Neither hath this man sinned, nor his parents: but that the works of God should be made manifest

in him.

⁴I must work the works of him that sent me, while it is day: the night cometh, when no man can work.

⁵As long as I am in the world, I am the light of the world.

John 9:3-5

You can only work the works of God while it is Day. We should work under the umbrella of revelation from the Word of God.

Writing is something I landed on by revelation and not by design. After going through some significant challenges for several months, I was in a park praying when a deep spirit of intercession hit me, and I went into what I call *"spiritual labour."* I continued in prayer until I felt a release like something coming out of me. Immediately after this, the exertion stopped, and God spoke to me to go and write. I have been writing ever since with signs following. I get book titles and outlines *"by accident."* When I asked Him how I was going to get the content for all the titles, He asked me a question, *"How many letters of the Alphabet are there?"* I answered, *"Twenty-Six."* He then said, *"Do you realise that all the books ever written in the English language came out of these twenty-six letters?"*

On another day, He brought to my remembrance that He was new every day from my standpoint. Therefore, if I write what I discover about Him every day, eternity cannot exhaust the amount of material available for me to write. Every time words like this enter my spirit, my Day gets brighter.

I have never sat down to write and wondered what to

write. The minute I touch the keyboard, the thoughts start to flow. The only reason this is happening is that I am working while it is Day. You may not understand the process, but you cannot deny the fact. People who work while it is Day always have superior results.

Job, one of the richest men who ever lived, was a man who understood what it meant to work in the DAY. The light he represented to the people was a reflection of the light he was receiving from God. How did Job navigate the darkness? He discovered how to get the light of God into the affairs of men. He knew that without the light of God, living life could be frustrating. God did not build us to leave life without His light.

> *²Oh that I were as in months past, as in the days when God preserved me;*
>
> *³When his candle shined upon my head, and when by his light I walked through darkness;*
>
> *⁴As I was in the days of my youth, when the secret of God was upon my tabernacle;*
>
> *Job 29:2-4*

Jesus focused on specific groups of people for His assignment and interestingly, Job embodied the same philosophy. Look at what he did with the light.

> *¹²Because I delivered the poor that cried, and the fatherless, and him that had none to help him.*
>
> *¹³The blessing of him that was ready to perish came upon me: and I caused the widow's heart to sing for joy.*
>
> *¹⁴I put on righteousness, and it clothed me: my judgment was as a robe and a diadem.*

¹⁵I was eyes to the blind, and feet was I to the lame.

¹⁶I was a father to the poor: and the cause which I knew not I searched out.

¹⁷And I brake the jaws of the wicked, and plucked the spoil out of his teeth.

Job 29:12-17

Job's motive was about meeting the needs of the people. He was to people what they could not be to themselves. Some people are so self-centred that the light of God is not shining through them. Consult with the Word of God and let this light lighten your darkness. With the light of God in you, you can create light out of darkness. Almost every highly productive person I have seen has at one time, or the other looked for the opportunity to connect with the inner light of God and have developed customs that keep them in this flow of light.

Work Needs Intermediate Products

God had specific, identifiable products for each day. If you cannot precisely define your intermediate or end product, you may struggle to apply your skills creatively. You can utilise your mind better, where you have more precise goals.

Notice that I refer to intermediate products. Words create sentences that create paragraphs. Paragraphs make chapters that develop into books. Once you have separated the Day from the Night, start to put the intermediate products together. Every big dream contains smaller intermediate dreams. These intermediate dreams play a very significant part in the overall process of working the talk. Firstly, they allow you to approach the next, more meaningful, step and overcome the value-cost proposition dilemma we talked about earlier.

Your intermediate product or service may require different skills which may mean you need other people to help with each stage. Very few people can help you at every stage of your life without having some parental oversight over you. Your parents follow every developmental stage of your life and still feel a sense of responsibility for you no matter your age until they die. This is a great price for someone to pay. Intermediate products lower the entry point for mentors who are vital agents of development.

Intermediate products also allow you to lose some without losing all. It reduces the impact of a domino effect. The only move you will need to remake is the last move. Reexamine your life and consider the areas you feel heavily burdened. Find out which intermediate products or services you can create. You are not making these intermediate products because God is limited; you are doing it because of the environment you live in. Drilling through rocks and drilling through sand require different drilling methods.

There is a crucial fact you need to bear in mind here. Your intermediate products need to be linked; otherwise, you will feel you have wasted time on irrelevant things in the past, which may lead to frustration. The things God created in Day 3 became very relevant in Day 6. As long as you are working under the light, while it is Day, your intermediate products may look disconnected externally, do not worry, they will reconnect.

Some years ago, I was working on a computer software development project and the person managing the project at the time had not been through the software development lifecycle on the scale at which we were addressing the task. I started with the database design and modelled their requirements by throwing different scenarios they had against this model. This went on for quite a while, and the manager started to get nervous that he had not seen any results, only diagrams on the wall. It was not until much later in the process when almost all the computer entry screens were being created by different people who were clear of what the screen they were working on was supposed to do, that he understood what I had been telling him. I focused on the data we had to capture and where to store it. I then focused on the data entry screens and what those had to look like.

With this approach, we delivered the project way ahead of time and budget. More importantly, the client was happy with the outcome. Build your present on your past successes. Even past failures could be propelling agents for present and future achievements. God has a way of helping you turn mistakes of the past into signposts that turn you in the direction of success.

Work Needs A Timely Order

Great workers make time relevant and are more prepared to take advantage of opportunities when they arrive. Not only is the timing of things important, the order in which they happen is also crucial. Within the context of this order, there are unlimited permutations that can be generated in enough variety to eliminate boredom. When building a house, the roof and the windows do not go in before the foundation and the walls. Altering the order of things in *Genesis 1* in any way destabilises the whole structure of creation.

Do not be pressured to make the external look more than it is. In due course, if you remain focused, the dots will connect. When building large buildings, the foundation typically goes deeper into the ground before the building starts to rise. Follow the principles line by line and before long, and the benefits will begin to roll in in leaps and bounds. Avoid the temptation to create the trappings of success before making the substance of success.

One very striking point about the order of creation is that the Bible describes each day as "*Evening and Morning.*" For me, this was a wake-up call, as I had always talked about morning and evening. So the order was quite alarming because we usually "*work*" during the day (morning) and "*rest*" at night (evening).

> [6]*And it shall come to pass in that day, that the light shall not be clear, nor dark:*
>
> [7]*But it shall be one day which shall be known to the LORD,*

not day, nor night: but it shall come to pass, that at evening time it shall be light.

⁸And it shall be in that day, that living waters shall go out from Jerusalem; half of them toward the former sea, and half of them toward the hinder sea: in summer and in winter shall it be.

Zechariah 14:6-8

I saw a different perspective of work from this. Spend the quiet hours of the night conceptualising and let the concepts sink into your subconscious as you sleep. Let your spirit gain control of these concepts and influence them without the interference of your mind. When you wake up, you start to put physical labour to the concepts until they materialise in tangible form.

⁵I have considered the days of old, the years of ancient times.

⁶I call to remembrance my song in the night: I commune with mine own heart: and my spirit made diligent search.

⁷Will the Lord cast off for ever? and will he be favourable no more?

Psalm 77:5-7

Why did the Psalmist's spirit diligently search in the night? I work late at night sometimes and in the early hours of the day at other times. From experience, it feels as if knowledge hides during the day and comes out at night looking for the diligent heart.

¹The heavens declare the glory of God; and the firmament sheweth his handywork.

²Day unto day uttereth speech, and night unto night sheweth knowledge.

³There is no speech nor language, where their voice is not heard.

Psalm 19:1-3

Take advantage of time, and God will teach you to number your days. There are enough hours in your life for the fulfilment of your dreams. Re-calibrate the body. If you travel to a country in a completely different time zone from yours, after some days, your body clock will reset. You can readjust your life to take advantage of time.

I watched a TV programme about what top pop celebrities do to stay at the top of their game. While their product, in some cases, may not agree with our theology, we cannot argue against the principles being used.

¹FOR ALL this I took to heart, exploring and examining it all, how the righteous (the upright, in right standing with God) and the wise and their works are in the hands of God. Whether it is to be love or hatred no man knows; all that is before them.

²All things come alike to all. There is one event to the righteous and to the wicked, to the good and to the clean and to the unclean; to him who sacrifices and to him who does not sacrifice. As is the good man, so is the sinner; and he who swears is as he who fears and shuns an oath.

Ecclesiastes 9:1-2 (AMP)

The principle for delivery is the same irrespective of theological convictions. The only difference is what happens with the life after the event. The memory of the wicked will be forgotten and they will end up in hell while the righteous will reign with God for eternity.

So when this timely order is violated we get chaos. Chaos is the manifestation of the violated order of work. If we do Christianity right, our places of fellowship can be one of the most advanced business schools in the world giving us the mental tools required to dominate our environment.

Chapter Key Points

Most failed projects do not fail in the big things, they fail in the simple things but simple issues not handled well become greater problems

You cannot become a professional without being a protégé

Thinking of cost first destroys creativity but thinking of value first triggers creativity

Do not be pressured to make the external look more than it really is. In due course, the dots will connect if you remain focused

Avoid the temptation to create the trappings of success before creating the substance of success